Pigs Aren't Dirty Bears Aren't Slow

And Other Truths About Misunderstood Animals

by Joanna Boutilier

art by Ben Hodson

ANNICK PRESS
TORONTO • NEW YORK • VANCOUVER

Contents

Introduction

Have you ever met the "big, bad wolf" in a story? Did you ever see a "wise old owl" in a poem or a movie? Have you ever heard the sayings "blind as a bat," "dirty pig," or "lazy lion"? Would you be surprised to learn that many of our ideas about animals are outdated, only half-right, or just plain wrong?

The earth, seas, and sky are full of amazing creatures. Most of them seem very different from us. They may be hairy, scaly, slippery, or slimy. Some of them eat things that  seem weird to us, such as insects, mice, garbage, dead animals, or sometimes even people. They may have a venomous sting or bite. Some have sharp, scary-looking teeth or claws. They may behave in ways that seem strange to us, such as rolling in the mud, shedding their skin all at once, or howling. We can easily misunderstand creatures that seem different from us, especially if we fear that they could harm us.

A wrong idea about something is called a misconception. Making mistakes and having misconceptions are natural parts of learning about the world. We frequently start with a wrong idea and then gradually improve our understanding as we learn more. As people study animals and their place in the world more closely, we are learning many exciting new things about animals, humans, and the special balance of nature on earth. We are discovering the fantastic diversity of animal life and the interdependence of all living things.

In this book you will learn about some of the common, weird, and wacky misconceptions people have about animals. We will uncover some of the amazing facts behind these misunderstandings.

Animals are fascinating creatures that are fun to observe. When we look closely, we are sure to be surprised and delighted and we may find that these animals are clever and useful in ways we had not imagined. We may also realize that animals are a valuable part of the web of life on earth. Learning about the earth and its creatures is a never-ending journey of discovery. Join the adventure and let's see what exciting facts and ideas we can learn about misunderstood animals.

Service to the Earth

Who is Afraid of the Big Bad Wolf?

Wolves are the largest members of the dog family. They are very intelligent, social animals who live in family packs. Each pack is led by a larger male and female wolf who mate for life. People sometimes think that all wolves are gray. However, like dogs, wolves come in different colors. Most wolves are a mix of brown, black, white, reddish-brown, or gray.

How many different colors can you see in this wolf's fur?

A common misunderstanding about wolves is that they are "bad" and they commonly hurt people, like the "big, bad wolf" from stories like "Little Red Riding Hood" or "The Three Little Pigs." You may be surprised to learn that wolves are normally very shy, retiring animals. Wolves actually fear humans and would much rather hide from us than confront us. The natural prey for wolves is deer, elk, bison, and moose—not people. Wolves hunt these animals not because they are mean or "bad," but only in order to survive.

Wolves certainly are powerful hunters. Little Red Riding Hood was obviously right about some things, for when she told the wolf that his teeth were very big, that was no misconception! Wolves have four large, sharp canine teeth that can grow to the size of your thumb. Their jaws are especially strong and can break

the neck of a deer with just one bite! Wolves can also run very fast. With such strength, speed, and skill as hunters, it is easy to see why people sometimes fear wolves.

Some people think that wolves continue to be a common and serious pest to many farmers, but this is not the case. As people have spread across the earth and taken over new lands, they have often moved into areas where wolves were living. When this happens, wolves will sometimes prey upon farm animals. This has led to conflict between wolves and people. As a result, there are many fewer wolves in the world nowadays and wolves are considered an endangered species. Most remaining wolves live far away from people in remote, wild areas.

Another misunderstanding about wolves is that they howl at the moon. Wolves do howl but not at the moon. Rather, howling is just one way for wolves to talk to each other. Sometimes they howl to talk to other wolves who are far away. Sometimes several wolves howl together in a way that almost seems like singing. Wolves also make many other noises, such as growling, whimpering, grunting, and barking.

Wilderness or bust?

Eensy Weensy Spider

Spiders are fascinating creatures who have crawled the earth for longer than people or dinosaurs. Spiders are busy spinning webs almost everywhere on earth – in deserts, fields, and forests, on mountains and in valleys, in your yard and inside your house. Many people mistakenly think that spiders are insects. Look closely at an insect, like an earwig or beetle, and you will see that it has six legs, three body parts (head, chest, and abdomen), antennae, and usually wings. Spiders are not insects, but arachnids. Spiders have eight legs, only two body parts (head and abdomen), plus a pair of small palpi near the spider's mouth. Palpi look like two short legs and work to catch and hold food. Spiders never have wings or antennae.

A common misconception about spiders is that they EAT their food. In fact, spiders cannot actually eat solid food at all. Instead, they DRINK their food! After catching an insect, spiders use their fangs to inject a special digestive juice into it. This juice turns the prey's insides to a soupy liquid, which the spider sucks out, leaving an empty shell. Spiders actually spend their whole lives on a liquid diet, drinking their meals in the form of a chunky soup or smoothie!

Mmm. Liquid Lunch.

Though wet, this spider's web can still catch insects.

Another common misunderstanding about spiders is that they are sly, venomous predators who like to bite people. However, of the 35,000 known species of spiders, only a few types are harmful to humans. In most cases, even venomous spiders hide from people and will bite only when threatened. However, you may be surprised to learn that there are people who like to bite spiders! The Piaroa people in the Amazon collect and eat large tarantulas, and in southeast Asia you can find women selling delicious barbecued spiders by the side of the road.

Some people also assume that large spiders are the most dangerous. Tarantulas, which are the largest spiders in North America, are often feared for this reason. In fact, the most dangerous spiders in North America are small. The black widow spider and the brown recluse spider have much stronger venom than tarantulas do. They are very shy, however, and try to hide from us as much as possible.

The world's many spiders are tremendously beneficial. They help to limit the insect pests that plague us by catching trillions of bugs, like flies and mosquitoes. Spiders are also a very important food for birds, as well as for some people!

This Little Piggy Went to Market

What ideas do you have about pigs? Many people think pigs are dirty, lazy, stupid, and greedy. People often dislike the way pigs eat, which is loudly and with gusto. Many people are also bothered by the way pigs behave, especially by the way they roll in the mud, grunt, and snort.

A pet pot-bellied pig crosses the street behind her owner.

Yet farmers and their families, who live and work with pigs, often have a lot of respect and fondness for them. Pigs are often treasured as one of the smartest animals on the farm. Experts have also found pigs to be as smart as dogs. Pigs are known for being able to remember things well and to use their keen sense of smell to locate things that are lost or buried underground. Many pigs also have a sweet nature and are sometimes kept as pets. In fact, pet pigs can be trained to do tricks, just like dogs. Pigs can learn to roll over, to fetch, to walk on a leash, to use a litter box, and to come when called. For this reason, pigs are becoming more and more popular as pets.

The idea that pigs are dirty is also a misunderstanding. Pigs are actually known to be one of the cleanest animals on the farm! When given a clean, spacious pen in which to live, pigs sleep in one area of the pen and use another area as their bathroom. They often choose the highest ground for their sleeping area, so that when it rains, no dirt from their bathroom is washed into their bedroom!

Another misconception is that all pigs are pink and live on farms. However, there are many different species of pigs, of various colors, sizes, and shapes, from white to pink to black to spotted. While it is certainly true that most pigs now live on farms, there are still some wild species of pigs that live in the forests of Europe, Asia, and Africa. Some of these pigs even have large tusks and look very different from the pigs that live on farms. The wart hog is an African pig with tusks on its head that can grow to be about as long as your arms!

Pigs also have a very good reason for wallowing in the mud. Pigs have sensitive skin. Under their skin, they have a thick layer of fat that warms them in winter but in summer makes them hot. Pigs can't sweat to cool off. Rolling in the mud to coat their skin is a natural way for pigs to stay cool. The mud also protects pigs from insects, such as the flies and mosquitoes that bother farm animals.

Snake in the Grass!

Snakes are amazing legless reptiles that can move on all surfaces except ice and snow. A common misunderstanding about snakes is that most snakes are harmful to people. In truth, over three-quarters of the snakes in the world are completely harmless to us. Most snakes actually fear people and try to hide from us. Only a small number of snakes have venom that is harmful to humans. There are 2,600 types of snakes in the world, in all colors and sizes. Some live in deserts, forests, caves, and burrows, others in rivers, lakes, and oceans. Some snakes are as tiny as your baby finger, while others are as long as a truck.

Some people also assume that snakes have no bones and that their body is just a head stuck to a long tail. In fact, snakes are vertebrates. This means they have a backbone, some-times a very long one indeed! Snakes also have a heart, lungs, and a stomach. In snakes, these organs are skinny and long, like the snake's body. Another misconception about snakes is that they are slimy. Like all reptiles, snakes have scaly skin. But a snake's skin is smooth, rather than slimy. If you look at the skin of a snake closely, it is really quite beautiful.

Can you see how well this snake blends with its habitat?

One of the oldest misunderstandings about snakes is that they are evil and mean. It is true that snakes often creep up on their prey very slowly, keeping their head and eyes pointed at the prey and staring with a steady, unblinking gaze. This has also led to the belief that snakes hypnotize their prey in some way. In fact, what may look like hypnotism is really just the snake's very careful method of hunting. A snake will also hide itself and lie completely still waiting for its prey to come near. The snake will then strike suddenly and capture the prey. This has led people to consider snakes to be evil or mean, when in fact this is a hunting method used by many animals, as well as people. Like many other animals, snakes hunt this way in order to survive, not because they are evil.

All over the world, snakes eat huge numbers of mice and rats every year. These rodents destroy crops and grain stores if unchecked. For this reason, some farmers protect snakes living near their farms. Even though we may sometimes fear them, snakes are a valuable part of our earth.

Nosey Bears

Most bears are enormous creatures, the largest remaining predator mammals on dry land. Many people think that bears live only in northern forests and on mountains. In fact, the eight different species of bears left in the world today live in many habitats, including hot, humid rain forests, swamps, deserts, tundra, and the freezing cold Arctic. The giant panda bear lives only in bamboo forests in China and the polar bear lives only in Arctic areas. Many people also think that all bears are huge. This is true in North America, where huge polar bears, American black bears, and brown bears roam. However, the sun bear, which lives in southern Asia, is only about the size of a large dog.

The Malayan sun bear loves honey and likes to sunbathe.

Not surprisingly, given that most bears are large predators, a common fear and misunderstanding about bears is that they often like to attack people. In fact, bears do not hunt humans as food. In the wild, nearly all bears naturally prefer to avoid people and, if possible, will even hide if they hear a person coming. However, if people enter a bear's territory and surprise or disturb it, a bear may strike to defend itself and its family.

Bear Buffet.

Many people have seen bears in national parks or garbage dumps and assume that these bears are safe to feed or pet. Surprisingly, this is not true. Although these bears have become accustomed to people, they are still wild animals. They have come to associate people with food and thus have lost their natural fear of humans. This actually makes them more dangerous to humans.

Another misconception is that bears are fat, clumsy, and slow. When searching for food or eating, bears can indeed seem slow and clumsy, but in fact they have very good balance and coordination. Bears can run with great speed when they need to, as fast as a horse for a short distance! All the more reason to remember that bears are wild animals that should never be approached, no matter how cute or tame they seem.

Many people also think that bears are mainly carnivorous, or meat-eating. Bears did evolve from carnivorous ancestors. However, today it is more accurate to describe most bears as omnivorous. Omnivores can and do eat flesh, but they also eat plants, insects, and many other foods. Most bears are wandering scavengers who eat almost everything they can find, including honey, berries, garbage, frogs, fish, birds, dead animals, insects, nuts, seeds, and rodents. Bears have an excellent sense of smell and are always nosing around trying to sniff out food.

Who Gives a Hoot About Owls?

Owls are fantastic birds of prey who have flown the earth for over 50 million years. Owls have large, staring eyes and often sit very still while quietly watching the world around them. This has led to the misconception that owls are very wise and intelligent. However, even compared with other birds, owls are not especially smart. Owls certainly are impressive creatures, but they are more remarkable for their great instincts, eyesight, hearing, and silent flight than for their intelligence.

Notice the powerful wings and talons of this amazing barred owl.

Most people know that owls have excellent night vision, but there is a common misconception that owls are blind in daylight. In fact, owls have huge, powerful eyes that see as well in daylight as they do at night. Compared to body size, if human eyes were as large as an owl's eyes, each of our eyes would be larger than a baseball! Although they can see in daylight, most owls hunt at night because this is when the rodents that they prey on are active.

Here comes lunch.

Speaking of eyesight, many people think that owls can rotate their heads in a complete circle to see in all directions. Owls are indeed able to see what is behind them, but they achieve this by turning their heads quickly from side to side about three-quarters of the way around each way.

Another misunderstanding is that owls mainly make hooting sounds. In fact, to mark their territory, warn intruders, or find a mate, owls make all sorts of different noises. They can hiss, moan, make laughing noises, and sound like monkeys. Sometimes, they make a terribly loud scream, which can be very frightening. Some species of owls do not even hoot at all!

You may wonder why we should give a hoot about owls. Owls are super hunters who have been called "winged cats" because they are even more skilled at catching rodents than cats are. Just one pair of barn owls can catch over a thousand mice for each brood of baby owls they raise! In this way, owls help to balance and control the rodent population wherever they live. Owls are great neighbors to have in your yard, in parks, in cities, and on farms.

Batty About Bats

Long ago, people thought that bats came out at night to hurt people and were evil witches' helpers. Today, most people do not believe in witches, but many still believe that bats may harm them. In fact, almost all bats are frightened of people and try to avoid us. Many people also believe that bats often carry a disease called rabies. Rabies is a serious sickness spread by the bite of an infected animal, which leads to death if not treated right away. However, humans rarely get rabies from bats. More common animals, such as dogs, cats, skunks, and raccoons, are actually far more likely to spread rabies than bats are.

African fruit bats huddle close together in their roosting cave.

Next time you hear the saying "blind as a bat" you may want to remember that this is a misconception too, for bats are not really blind at all. Bats that hunt in daylight usually have larger, stronger eyes. Night-hunting bats have weaker eyes. They rely mostly on a special radar hearing power to navigate and find food. This power is called echolocation, which means finding things using a sound and its echo. Echolocation is an amazing skill that is unique to bats.

Hmm....flies like a bird but hairy like a mammal.

Since bats can fly, people often think they are a type of bird. In fact, bats are truly unique creatures, since they are the only mammals that can fly. Like other mammals, bats are warm-blooded and give birth to live babies. Bats also have body hair or fur. Birds are warm-blooded vertebrates of the class Aves but are not mammals. Birds lay eggs and have feathers instead of hair or fur.

Another common misunderstanding about bats is that they are all black and scary-looking. In fact, there are nearly one thousand different types of bats and they come in all different colors and sizes. The tiny hog-nosed bat weighs only about as much as a dime, while the large flying fox bat has a wingspan as wide as a child's bed. Some bats eat insects, others eat fruits, and others feed on the nectar from flowers. Some bats have large eyes, puffy cheeks, and look as cute as a teddy bear.

Bats are incredible creatures who help the earth immensely. Bats devour billions of mosquitoes, flies, beetles, and worms each year. Some farmers now install bat houses in their orchards and fields so that more bats will come to eat the pests that damage crops. Bats also help to pollinate many flowers and to spread the seeds of many fruits so that new fruit will grow.

Sharks:
Wolves of the Sea

Sharks are tremendous predators, sometimes called "wolves of the sea" because they often gather together for hunting, feeding, and mating. A common misconception about sharks is that they are primitive, simple, and mindless creatures. Sharks are indeed ancient creatures, originating around 400 million years ago, which is 200 million years before the time of the dinosaurs. However, the fact that sharks are very old is not a sign that they are simple or lack intelligence. Some sharks have relatively large brains and have shown they can learn as quickly as birds and rats.

A white underbelly and gray upper body helps the great white shark to be camouflaged in the water from both above and below.

Sharks also have amazing abilities to detect prey, by using smell, hearing, touch, and taste, and by detecting vibrations and movements. They also have a special ability to sense the electric fields given off by their prey.

Many people think of sharks as huge, saw-toothed, blue-gray killers shaped like torpedoes. You may be surprised to learn that there are actually 368 different known species of sharks. Most sharks are smaller than your arm and quite harmless to humans. Some are as tiny as a candy bar, though others can be as large as a school bus. Sharks come in many colors, including brown, yellow, green, black,

Heading north
for the winter.

cream, and orange. Some types of sharks really are dangerous and should always be avoided. These include the great white, the bull shark, and oceanic whitetip shark. On the rare occasions when these sharks attack people, it is usually because they have mistaken a person for a seal, sea-lion, or other creature that is their normal prey.

Another common misunderstanding about sharks is that they live only in warm saltwater oceans. In fact, sharks roam widely throughout the oceans of the world, from warm, southern areas to cold, northern areas, from shallow, coastal areas to the deep ocean bottom, from coral reefs to the open waters in the middle of the ocean. Sharks are even found in icy arctic waters! The Greenland shark, blue shark, and basking shark all swim in the waters near the Arctic Circle. It is also true that most sharks live in salt-water, but there are a few species that can swim up rivers and even into freshwater lakes. The bull shark has been found miles upriver from the ocean in many large rivers, such as the Mississippi, the Amazon, and the Ganges.

People are often confused about whether sharks are mammals, fish, or some other type of creature. All fish have backbones and gills. Sharks are a special type of fish whose skeletons are made of cartilage rather than hard bone. Cartilage is a firm, flexible material similar to that found in your nose and outer ear.

The Lowly Toad

Many people believe that toads are ugly. But if you look closely, toads have a special beauty. Their skin is a lovely mix of dark colors, such as green, gray, brown, and black. This coloring helps them to hide from their enemies by blending with their surroundings. Toads like to live and hide in ponds, swamps, lakes, fields, gardens, and by the sides of rivers.

Notice how this toad's skin is the same colors as its surroundings.

One common misconception about toads is that touching a toad can give you warts. Toads do have bumps on their skin, but touching these bumps does not give you warts. Some of these bumps are simply natural ridges. Others are special glands that help the toad to protect itself from attackers by giving off a bitter, poisonous liquid that tastes horrible to other creatures. However, this liquid won't give you warts either. Warts are really caused by a virus that is not carried by toads. But the liquid certainly tastes awful if you lick the toad or try to eat it. Perhaps this is why people eat frogs' legs but not toads' legs! In any case, it is always a good idea to wash your hands after handling toads in order to remove any traces of this poisonous liquid from your hands.

Not just another pretty face.

Another misunderstanding about toads is that they urinate on you if you handle them. Toads have thin skin that allows their bodies to absorb and release water easily. When you pick up a toad, it is true that it often releases something wet on your hand, but this is not urine. Rather, it is water that the toad had stored up in its body for future use during dry or hot conditions. However, when the toad is frightened (by a big kid like you picking it up!), fear can cause its body to release this water.

Many people do not think much about toads, and when they do, they consider toads to be unimportant little creatures. You might wonder why we should care about lowly creatures like toads. The truth is that toads are incredibly beneficial and important creatures. Just like bats, snakes, and spiders, toads actually do a very important job. They eat lots and lots of harmful pests, such as flies, mosquitoes, crickets, locusts, aphids, beetles, ants, and slugs. Toads are great creatures to have in the farmer's field or in your backyard garden, since they eat a lot of the same pests that damage crops and gardens. An average American toad can eat up to 90 flies in just a couple of hours. Could you top that? More toads would be a good thing for all of us, toads and people alike, though not for mosquitoes and flies, of course.

33

The Lion's Share

Lions are wonderful, unique creatures. They are the only highly social cats, who live together in groups called prides. Male lions are the only members of the entire cat family with a mane, which is a marker of strength and power. A common misunderstanding about lions is that they live only on the grassy plains of Africa. However, lions will roam wherever there is enough prey to feed on, from open woodland, thick bush, and grassy plains, to desert and mountainous areas. Lions feed mostly on zebras, wildebeest, gazelles, and impalas, but will eat anything they can find.

Like cats, mother lions carry their cubs in their mouth.

Another misunderstanding about lions is that they often hunt humans. It is not surprising that people would fear lions, given their great speed and terrific hunting ability. Even so, lions usually avoid people when given the chance. Lions hunt only to feed themselves and it is much more common for lions to starve to death due to lack of food than it is for them to prey upon people.

People often think that lions are lazy. No doubt this is based on the fact that lions spend up to twenty hours of their day resting, sleeping, and just lounging around. Most African lions live in hot conditions and need to conserve their energy during the heat of

Let's hurry, those zebras are only a mile ahead now.

the day. Thus, most lions usually rest by day and rouse to hunt by night, when it is cooler. When lions are not resting, they are very active, often traveling 5 to 10 kilometers daily in search of food.

A common misconception is that male lions are the main hunters in a pride. It is true that male lions are much larger and stronger than females. However, female lions do most of the hunting, as they are faster and more agile. Since female lions do not have a big, bushy mane, it is also easier for females to sneak up on their prey. Males are more likely to patrol and defend the pride's territory. When it comes time to eat, however, the male lion goes first and gets "the lion's share" of whatever has been caught. Female lions feed next, followed by cubs.

Lions are also unique among cats in their ability to roar. Lions roar to mark their territory and warn intruders, to signal their position to other lions, and to release tension. For this reason, people sometimes think roaring is the only noise lions make. In fact, lions have many different noises, including grunting, snarling, hissing, yowling, and sighing. Some people also believe that lions can purr like domestic cats. Although lions are not known to purr like pet cats, they do "meow" like kittens when they are young cubs.

Further Reading

Wolves

Wood, Lily and Carolyn Otto. *Wolves.* Scholastic Science Readers Series. New York: Scholastic, 2001. (Age Level 7 – 8)

Brandenburg, Jim and Joann Bren Guernsey. *To the Top of the World: Adventures with Arctic Wolves.* New York: Walker & Company, 1995. (Age Level 8 and up)

Lawrence, R.D. *Wolves,* Vol. 1. Wildlife Library Series. New York: Little, Brown & Company, 2004. (Age Level 9 – 12)

Spiders

Murawski, Darlyne A. *Spiders and Their Webs.* Washington: National Geographic Society, 2004. (Age Level 6 – 11)

Berger, Melvin and Gilda Berger. *Do All Spiders Spin Webs? Questions and Answers About Spiders.* New York: Scholastic, 2000. (Age Level 8 – 11)

Pigs

Older, Jules. *Pig.* Watertown, MA: Charlesbridge Publishing, 2004. (Age Level 6 – 11)

Boyer Binns, Tristan. *Potbellied Pigs.* Keeping Unusual Pets Series. Portsmouth, NH: Heinemann, 2004. (Age Level 8 – 12)

Snakes

Mudd-Ruth, Maria. *Snakes.* Animals Animals Series. London: Marshall Cavendish, 2001. (Age Level 8 – 10)

Montgomery, Sy. *The Snake Scientist.* Scientists in the Field Series. Boston: Houghton Mifflin, 2001. (Age Level 9 – 11)

Bears

Schwabacher, Martin. *Bears.* Animals Animals Series. London: Marshall Cavendish, 2000. (Age Level 8 – 10)

Swinburne, Stephen R. *Black Bear: North America's Bear.* Honesdale, PA: Boyds Mills Press, 2004. (Age Level 8 – 12)

Owls

Swanson, Diane. *Owls.* Welcome to the World of Animals Series. Milwaukee, WI: Gareth Stevens Publishing, 1998. (Age Level 8 – 10)

Bats

Stuart, Dee. *Bats: Mysterious Flyers of the Night.* Nature Watch Series. Minneapolis, MN: Lerner Publishing Group, 1994. (Age Level 8 – 11)

Gibbons, Gail. *Bats.* New York: Holiday House, 2000. (Age Level 9 – 12)

Sharks

Cerullo, Mary M. *The Truth about Great White Sharks.* Truth about Series. San Francisco: Chronicle Books, 2000. (Age Level 8 – 11)

Mallory, Kenneth and New England Aquarium Staff. *Swimming with Hammerhead Sharks.* Scientists in the Field Series. Boston: Houghton Mifflin, 2001. (Age Level 9 – 11)

Toads

Swanson, Diane. *Frogs and Toads.* Welcome to the World of Animals Series. Milwaukee, WI: Gareth Stevens Publishing, 2003. (Age Level 7 – 10)

Lions

Kalman, Bobbie and Amanda Bishop. *Life Cycle of a Lion.* Life Cycles Series. New York: Crabtree Publishing Company, 2002. (Age Level 8 – 11)

Schafer, Susan. *Lions.* Animals Animals Series. London: Marshall Cavendish, 2000. (Age Level 8 – 10)

Name That

There are only a few remaining types of wolves left in the world.

Arctic Wolf

Gray Wolf

Mexican Wolf

Black Widow Spider

Garden Orbweaver Spider

European Garden Spider

Water Spider

Trapdoor Spider

Jumping Spider

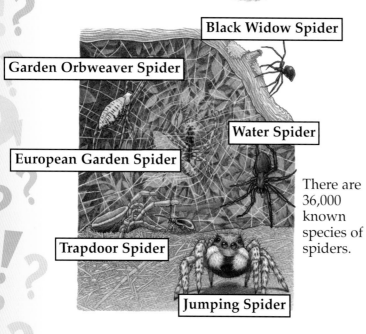

There are 36,000 known species of spiders.

There are up to 16 species of pigs.

Wild Boar

Domestic Pig

Wart Hog

Amazon Tree Boa

Garter Snake

There are over 2,600 species of snakes.

Copperhead Snake

Water Moccassin Snake

Arizona King Snake

There are 8 remaining species of bears in the world.

American Black Bear

Grizzly Bear

Giant Panda Bear

Polar Bear

Creature

There are over 130 species of owls.

Barn Owl

Northern Hawk Owl

Elf Owl

Snowy Owl

Eastern Screech Owl

Great Gray Owl

There are over 925 species of bats.

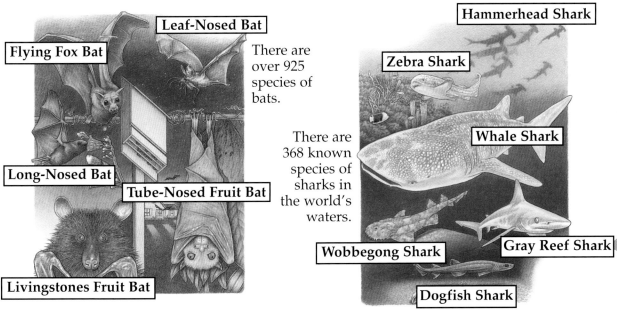

Flying Fox Bat

Leaf-Nosed Bat

Long-Nosed Bat

Tube-Nosed Fruit Bat

Livingstones Fruit Bat

Hammerhead Shark

Zebra Shark

There are 368 known species of sharks in the world's waters.

Whale Shark

Wobbegong Shark

Gray Reef Shark

Dogfish Shark

There are over 300 species of toads.

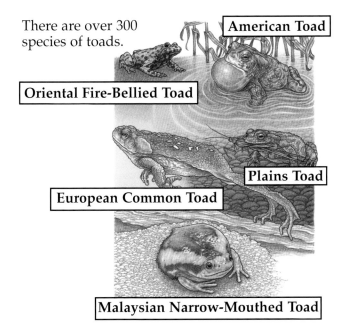

American Toad

Oriental Fire-Bellied Toad

Plains Toad

European Common Toad

Malaysian Narrow-Mouthed Toad

There are only two types of lions left in the world, the African lion and the Asiatic lion.

African lions

We acknowledge the support of the Canada Council for the Arts, the Ontario Arts Council, and the Government of Canada through the Book Publishing Industry Development Program (BPIDP) for our publishing activities.

Cataloging in Publication

Boutilier, Joanna
Pigs aren't dirty, bears aren't slow : and other truths about misunderstood animals / by Joanna Boutilier ; art by Ben Hodson.

Includes bibliographical references.
ISBN 1-55037-849-X (bound).—ISBN 1-55037-848-1 (pbk.)

1. Animals—Juvenile literature. I. Hodson, Ben II. Title.

QL49.B69 2005   j590   C2004-906669-2

The art in this book was rendered in pencil crayon.
The text was typeset in Palatino and Baileywick JF-Festive.

Distributed in Canada by:
Firefly Books Ltd.
66 Leek Crescent
Richmond Hill, ON
L4B 1H1

Published in the U.S.A. by
Annick Press (U.S.) Ltd.
Distributed in the U.S.A. by:
Firefly Books (U.S.) Inc.
P.O. Box 1338
Ellicott Station
Buffalo, NY 14205

Printed in China.

Visit us at: www.annickpress.com

Photo Credits

4, Scott Bauer, U.S. Department of Agriculture: Agricultural Research Service, K7623-1; 5 upper, Ardo X. Meyer, NOAA (ret.), anim0428, NOAA's Ark (Animals) Collection; 5 lower, Captain Budd Christman, NOAA Corps, anim0007, NOAA's Ark (Animals) Collection; 7, U.S. Department of Agriculture, 94cs3412; 12, AP/Wide World Photos, Durant Daily Democrat, Chris Jennings; 13, AP/Wide World Photos, Dana Fisher; 18, NOAA National Estuarine Research Reserve Collection, nerr0380; 19, AP/Wide World Photos, Frank Rumpenhorst; 22, AP/Wide World Photos, Jeff Barnard; 25, Roger De La Harpe; Gallo Images/CORBIS/Magma; 28, AP/Wide World Photos, Tom Uhlman; 31, Entheos, Environmental Protection Agency, U. S. National Archives & Records Administration NWDNS-412-DA-12615; 34, AP/Wide World Photos, Diether Endlicher

For Misha, Sasha, and Jason
—J.B.

To my family for their support, and to all the creatures of the world, large and small, who are misunderstood.
—B.H.